D0338295

Dear Parents and Educators,

Welcome to Penguin Young Readers! As parents and educators, you know that each child develops at his or her own pace—in terms of speech, critical thinking, and, of course, reading. Penguin Young Readers recognizes this fact. As a result, each Penguin Young Readers book is assigned a traditional easy-to-read level (1–4) as well as a Guided Reading Level (A–P). Both of these systems will help you choose the right book for your child. Please refer to the back of each book for specific leveling information. Penguin Young Readers features esteemed authors and illustrators, stories about favorite characters, fascinating nonfiction, and more!

## Martin Luther King Jr. and the March on Washington

**LEVEL 3**

GUIDED READING LEVEL **M**

This book is perfect for a **Transitional Reader** who:
• can read multisyllable and compound words;
• can read words with prefixes and suffixes;
• is able to identify story elements (beginning, middle, end, plot, setting, characters, problem, solution); and
• can understand different points of view.

Here are some **activities** you can do during and after reading this book:
• Nonfiction: Nonfiction books deal with facts and events that are real. Talk about the elements of nonfiction. Discuss some of the facts you learned about Martin Luther King Jr. and the March on Washington.
• Creative Writing: In his famous "I Have a Dream" speech, Martin Luther King Jr. describes specific hopes he has for the future. Write your own speech detailing something you feel passionate about. What dreams do you have for the future?

Remember, sharing the love of reading with a child is the best gift you can give!

—Bonnie Bader, EdM
  Penguin Young Readers program

*Penguin Young Readers are leveled by independent reviewers applying the standards developed by Irene Fountas and Gay Su Pinnell in *Matching Books to Readers: Using Leveled Books in Guided Reading*, Heinemann, 1999.

For my father and in
memory of my mother
—FER

For Mary, John, Daisy,
and Gary, good friends all
—SM

Penguin Young Readers
Published by the Penguin Group
Penguin Group (USA) Inc., 375 Hudson Street, New York, New York 10014, USA
Penguin Group (Canada), 90 Eglinton Avenue East, Suite 700, Toronto, Ontario M4P 2Y3, Canada
(a division of Pearson Penguin Canada Inc.)
Penguin Books Ltd., 80 Strand, London WC2R 0RL, England
Penguin Group Ireland, 25 St. Stephen's Green, Dublin 2, Ireland (a division of Penguin Books Ltd.)
Penguin Group (Australia), 250 Camberwell Road, Camberwell, Victoria 3124, Australia
(a division of Pearson Australia Group Pty. Ltd.)
Penguin Books India Pvt. Ltd., 11 Community Centre, Panchsheel Park, New Delhi—110 017, India
Penguin Group (NZ), 67 Apollo Drive, Rosedale, Auckland 0632, New Zealand
(a division of Pearson New Zealand Ltd.)
Penguin Books (South Africa) (Pty.) Ltd., 24 Sturdee Avenue,
Rosebank, Johannesburg 2196, South Africa

Penguin Books Ltd., Registered Offices: 80 Strand, London WC2R 0RL, England

All rights reserved. No part of this book may be reproduced, scanned, or distributed in any printed or
electronic form without permission. Please do not participate in or encourage piracy of copyrighted
materials in violation of the author's rights. Purchase only authorized editions.

Text copyright © 2001 by Frances E. Ruffin. Illustrations copyright © 2001 by Stephen Marchesi.
All rights reserved. First published in 2001 by Grosset & Dunlap, an imprint of Penguin Group (USA) Inc.
Published in 2012 by Penguin Young Readers, an imprint of Penguin Group (USA) Inc.,
345 Hudson Street, New York, New York 10014. Printed in the U.S.A.

Library of Congress Control Number: 00057304

ISBN 978-0-448-42421-7                    10 9 8 7 6 5 4

ALWAYS LEARNING                                            PEARSON

# MARTIN LUTHER KING JR.

## and the March on Washington

WITHDRAWN

by Frances E. Ruffin
illustrated by Stephen Marchesi

Penguin Young Readers
An Imprint of Penguin Group (USA) Inc.

# August 28, 1963

It is a hot summer day in
Washington, DC.

More than 250,000 people are
pouring into the city.

They have come by plane, by train,
by car, and by bus.

Some people have walked all the way
to Washington from New York City.
That's more than 230 miles.

One man has roller-skated
from Chicago.
It has taken him 11 days!

By late morning, a crowd has
gathered at one end of a long,
narrow pool.

Nearby is the Lincoln Memorial
with its statue of Abraham Lincoln.

Why are so many people here
at this place on this day?

It is because one hundred years ago, President Lincoln helped to free the people who were slaves.

It was during the Civil War.

President Lincoln knew that slavery had to end.

Now it is 1963.

There has been no slavery for a long time.

But are black people and white people treated equally?

No.

And that is why people are in Washington today.

They have come to protest.

They will speak out against something they think is wrong.

In the South and in some other states, there are laws to keep black people and white people apart.

Black people cannot eat in many restaurants or stay in many hotels.

In movie theaters, they must enter
by separate doors and sit way up in
the balcony.

On public buses, they have to take seats in the back.

There are signs that say,
"For Whites Only."
Even water fountains say
"White" or "Colored."

Which of these fountains
looks nicer to you?

Black people and many white people want things to change. It is time for a change. It is *past* time for a change.

In the crowd are some grandchildren
and great-grandchildren of slaves.
Many of these people have been
part of protests before.

UAW SAYS!
END
SEGREGATED
RULES
IN
PUBLIC
SCHOOLS

I.U.E
FOR
FULL
EMPLOYMENT

There have been sit-ins in many cities.

At sit-ins, black people take seats in

"white only" restaurants or theaters.

And they refuse to leave.

Often they are dragged out.

Sometimes they are put in jail.

There have been protest marches
in many Southern cities and towns.

People hold signs.

They sing songs.

But what if everyone got together in one place to protest?

That is the idea of two black leaders named A. Philip Randolph and Bayard Rustin.

They pick Washington, DC, as the place. It is the nation's capital. It is where laws are made.

So, on August 28, 1963, at 11:30 AM, the March on Washington begins.

The crowd marches to the Lincoln Memorial.

As they walk, the people sing:

*We shall overcome,*

*We shall overcome,*

*We shall overcome someday.*

Later, there are many speakers.
They stand on the steps of the
memorial, in front of Lincoln's statue.
Each person talks about freedom.
The marchers sit on the grass
and listen. They know that today
history is being made.

By noon, the sun is very hot.

Some people take off their shoes and cool their feet in the pool.

Bag lunches are sold. Each one has a cheese sandwich, an apple, and a slice of pound cake—all for 50 cents.

The high point of the day comes at
three o'clock.

The crowd grows quiet.

A young black man takes the stage.

He looks at the crowd. There are
people as far as he can see.

The man's name is Martin Luther King Jr.

He is a preacher and the son of a preacher.

He has grown up in Georgia. He knows all about what it is like to be a black person in the South.

Dr. King is a man of peace.

But he is also a fighter.

He doesn't use his fists or weapons.

He uses words.

In the South, Dr. King has led many other protests.

One was a march in Georgia.

Another was a protest against a bus company in Alabama.

He has been put in jail many times.

There are threats against his life.
Some people want him dead.
But that does not stop him.
Today, in Washington, Dr. King
speaks words of hope. His speech is
about his dream for a better world.

He says, "I have a dream that my four little children will one day live in a nation where they will not be judged by the color of their skin . . ."

He hopes that people will see all children for who they are and for the things they do in their lives.

It is his dream that one day "little black boys and black girls will be able to join hands with little white boys and girls."

Dr. King speaks for 16 minutes and 20 seconds.

His voice rises and falls.

The crowd leans forward.

They want to hear every word.

Nine times Dr. King says, "I have a dream."

When Dr. King finishes, there
is silence.

Then 250,000 people start to clap
and to cheer. Some people are so
moved by his words, they cry.

People all around the world watch
Martin Luther King Jr. on TV.
So does President John F. Kennedy.

By early evening, people start back to their cars, to the buses, and to the trains and planes.

It is time to go home. The march has ended.

But that is not the end of the story.

One year later, a law is passed.

It is called the Civil Rights Act of 1964.

From now on, there cannot be restaurants for "whites only."

There cannot be separate seating for black people and white people in any public place.

People cannot be kept apart just because of their skin color.

It does not change everything.

But it is a beginning.

And the power of words, the words of Dr. King and others, changes the law of the land.

3 1901 05468 8637